Design and Make Your Own Floral Appliqué

WITH FULL-SIZE TEMPLATES AND STEP-BY-STEP INSTRUCTIONS

Eva Costabel-Deutsch

DOVER PUBLICATIONS, INC.
NEW YORK

Published in Canada by General Publishing
Company, Ltd., 30 Lesmill Road, Don Mills,
Toronto, Ontario.
Published in the United Kingdom by Con-
stable and Company, Ltd., 10 Orange Street,
London WC2H 7EG.

*Design and Make Your Own Floral Appliqué,
with Full-Size Templates and Step-by-Step Instructions* is a new work, first published by Dover
Publications, Inc., in 1976.

*International Standard Book Number:
0-486-23427-4
Library of Congress Catalog Card Number:
76-24568*

Manufactured in the United States of America
Dover Publications, Inc.
180 Varick Street
New York, N. Y. 10014

❧ Introduction ❧

It is hard to imagine a needlework form more appropriate for the modern embroiderer than the ancient form of appliqué embroidery. Appliqué is quick, easy and economical. In terms of completed projects per working hours, appliqué is far ahead of any other embroidery form. Even a beginner can achieve lovely designs; yet appliqué offers a challenge to the most sophisticated needleworker because it provides so many opportunities for individuality. Any scrap of fabric may be used for an appliqué project: small pieces of material left over from another sewing project, washed-out fabrics, old lace, bits of crochet, scraps of fur.

Appliqué can be used for any project that you might normally make with other forms of embroidery: pillows, wall-hangings, eyeglass cases, tablecloths, purses, and so forth. Bits of appliqué can be used to decorate clothes and home furnishings, and appliqué has for years been used to decorate quilts.

This book constitutes a unique and simple method of doing appliqué embroidery. With its aid the embroiderer who enjoys doing appliqué but does not know how to draw can create many lovely pieces.

There are seven completed floral appliqué embroidery pieces photographed on the covers of this book. All of the component shapes used in making these appliqués are given in actual-size templates printed on special heavyweight paper. Diagrams showing which shapes have been used to make each appliqué appear on pages 7–12. You can reproduce the appliqué as it appears in the photograph by using the appropriate templates indicated on the diagram. Add your own individual touches by your selection of color and fabrics and by the addition of your own choice of embroidery stitches.

Since all of the component pieces are interchangeable, you can be even more creative by making your own unique appliqué. Choose a leaf from one design, a petal from another, a complete flower form from a third design. Combine your floral arrangement in a container from another design. There are three basic approaches to creating a unique piece of needlework:

1. Making a sketch and planning ahead, carefully choosing which templates will be used.

2. Working spontaneously by moving the shapes around until a pleasing composition is reached.

3. Combining the planned-in-advance method with flexibility and spontaneity.

The choice of which technique you use is yours since different personalities approach projects in different ways. In the end, the result is the same; you will have produced a work of art that will be pleasing to you.

This book is not intended to be a detailed instruction book on appliqué embroidery; that subject is already well covered in numerous inexpensive books (one of which is *Appliqué Old and New*, by Nedda C. Anders, a Dover paperback reprint, 0-486-23246-8, $2.50). In this brief introduction, however, I should like to review some of the basic methods you will need to create any of the seven appliqué designs on the covers.

Materials

FABRICS

Try to see that the fabric to be used for the appliqué shapes and the fabric to be used for the background are similar to one another in weight and texture. For instance, organdy applied to wool will probably not produce a pleasing result. In addition, if possible choose fabrics for the shapes which don't fray when cut. If you want to use some of the more delicate fabrics, follow the special instructions on how to deal with easily fraying fabrics on page five. In general, the following fabrics are the easiest to work with: cotton, silk, linen, felt, chintz, wool, velvet, brocade, sailcloth, canvas and duck. Felt has a unique place in appliqué and is one of my favorite fabrics. Since there is no need for seam allowance, shapes can be more accurate and many embroidery stitches can be used to attach the shapes to the backround. Felt is now available in bright, clear colors—very appropriate for modern design. Since with felt there is no concern about right or wrong side, or top or bottom, it is most economical to use as there is never any waste.

EMBROIDERY THREADS

Use threads that correspond in kind and weight to the fabrics you are using. For instance, use mercerized and cotton threads on cottons and linens; silks and synthetics on silks and velvets. Embroidery wools are very useful for adding bold effects to your design.

NEEDLES

Use embroidery needles for fine and medium weight fabrics and threads. Chenille needles can be used for heavier fabrics and threads. If your needle discolors or if it becomes difficult to pull through fabric, this may be due to oxidation. Needles are made of steel, and the constant perspiration of your hands can cause this phenomenon. It is not necessary to throw the needle away; just poke it through a sawdust pincushion.

STRAIGHT PINS

A good supply of pins is helpful to keep appliqué shapes secured to the background while you are putting your design together.

SCISSORS

You will need a sharp scissors with pointed blades which close perfectly for cutting out the appliqué shapes. You will also find an embroidery scissors with a sharp point helpful for cutting the embroidery threads.

THIMBLE

The use of a thimble is purely a matter of choice. While it is not a necessity in any form of embroidery, a thimble will protect your finger from getting sore, especially when you are working with stiff fabrics. If you simply cannot work with a thimble, you might try covering your middle and index fingers with tape to protect them.

EMBROIDERY FRAMES AND HOOPS

While most appliqué can be embroidered in the hands, you may prefer to stretch large projects in a frame. Keep the frame slack until the pieces are sewn in place, then tighten the frame when you begin to do the more intricate embroidery. You can also use an embroidery hoop, moving the hoop onto each section as you work. The use of frames and hoops will be an aid in keeping the fabric from puckering.

OTHER MATERIALS

You will find some or all of these materials helpful: clear-drying glue suitable for fabrics, soft pencil, X-acto knife, single-edged razor blade, ruler, iron and trimmings such as cords, ribbons and braids.

Beginning the Work

1. From the photographs on the cover, select the appliqué design that you wish to make.

2. Following the diagrams on pages 7 - 12, locate the designated templates and carefully cut them out. To keep the edges of the cardboard as neat and firm as possible, use a large scissors, a single-edged razor blade or an X-acto knife. Since these templates are all reusable, you may want to keep all of the templates together for each appliqué.

3. Cut the background fabric, allowing an additional 1″ to 1½″ hem all around. If you intend to turn your appliqué design into a wall hanging, allow additional fabric for rod casings at the top and bottom.

4. Select the fabrics that you will use for the appliqué shapes, as discussed in the previous section. If the fabric for the background and the shapes have different weaves, it is a good idea to preshrink the fabrics by washing them before proceeding further. This will eliminate any wrinkling problem should one fabric shrink more than the others.

5. Iron the fabric.

Cutting and Preparing the Shapes

The templates do not have seam allowance indicated on them. Whether seam allowance must be added depends upon the method you will use to apply the shapes to the background. If you choose to use method I (see below), allow ⅛″ to ¼″ seam allowance before cutting the shape. Method II (see below) requires no seam allowance. If you are working with felt, seam allowance is never required.

1. Lay the template on the wrong side of the material and carefully mark around the template with a pencil.

2. If you want a seam allowance, cut ⅛″ to ¼″ outside this pencil line. If you do not want a seam allowance, cut on the pencil line.

3. Shapes with seam allowance will require special preparation. While there are various methods you may use, the following two are especially simple:

    (a) Put the appliqué shape on the ironing board, wrong side up. Lay the template in the center of the piece, inside the seam allowance. Iron the seam-allowance portion over the template. Remove the template and press again.

    (b) Crease the seam allowance with your finger nail and fold under. Baste.

Whichever method you use, it may be necessary to clip round shapes into the pencil mark (not quite all the way) to get the shape to lie smooth.

4. Place a hot iron on the shape and press down. Do not put the iron around the edges because this may stretch the shape. Use steam if necessary, but the shape must be well pressed before it is applied to the background.

Applying the Shapes to the Background

(METHOD I)

1. Lay the shapes on the background fabric, moving them around until the desired composition is obtained.

2. Pin or baste into position; using the center of the shape, leaving the outer edge for embroidery stitches. If you are working with large shapes and are having trouble holding them down, put a *thin* coat of paste over the center of the background *only* before putting down the shape.

3. The shapes are permanently anchored to the background with a stitch of your own choice. Most traditional appliqués were done with an invisible slip stitch, a hemming stitch or a tiny whip stitch. This is still a popular method of appliqué. If you choose this method, use a fine thread that is the same color as the shape. Another very popular technique is to go around the piece with embroidery floss using various embroidery stitches or a simple running stitch. The running stitch is usually done with a contrasting thread and is placed about ⅛″ inside the edge of the shape. The thread used for the embroidery stitches or the running stitch becomes itself a decorative part of the appliqué. In the appliqué on the front cover of this book, the pitcher was applied with a whip stitch, the orange tulip with a running stitch and the white flower with chain stitch. The leaf appliqué on the back cover

INSTRUCTIONS CONTINUE AFTER TEMPLATES

A3

A2

A4

A1

A5

PLATE A

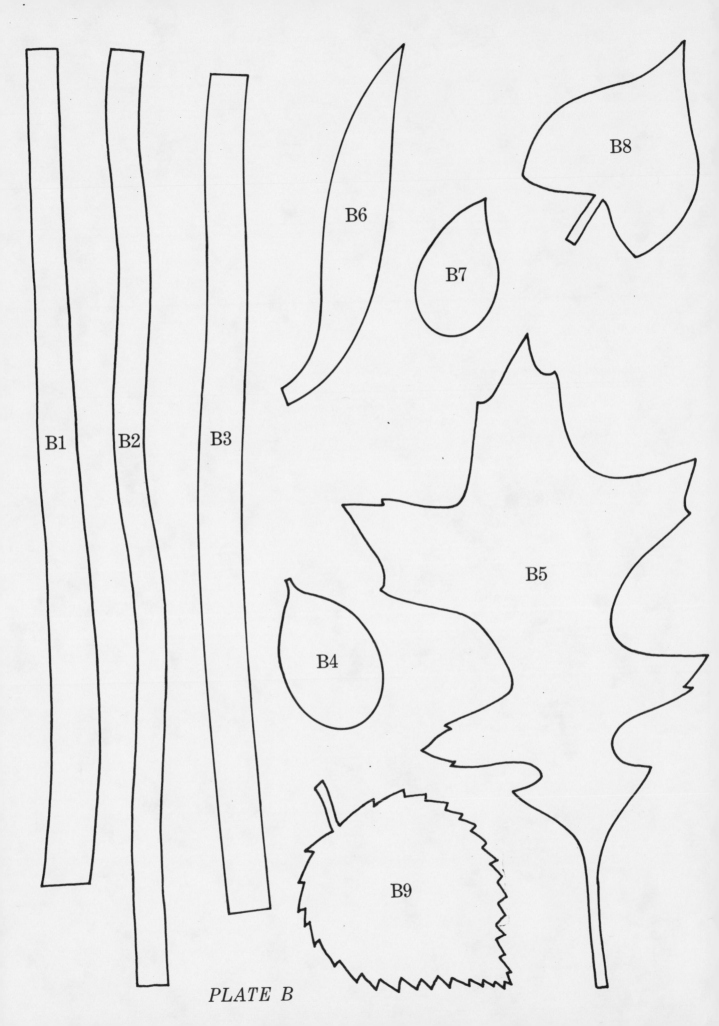

B1

B2

B3

B6

B7

B8

B4

B5

B9

PLATE B

C2

C1

C3

C4

C5

PLATE C

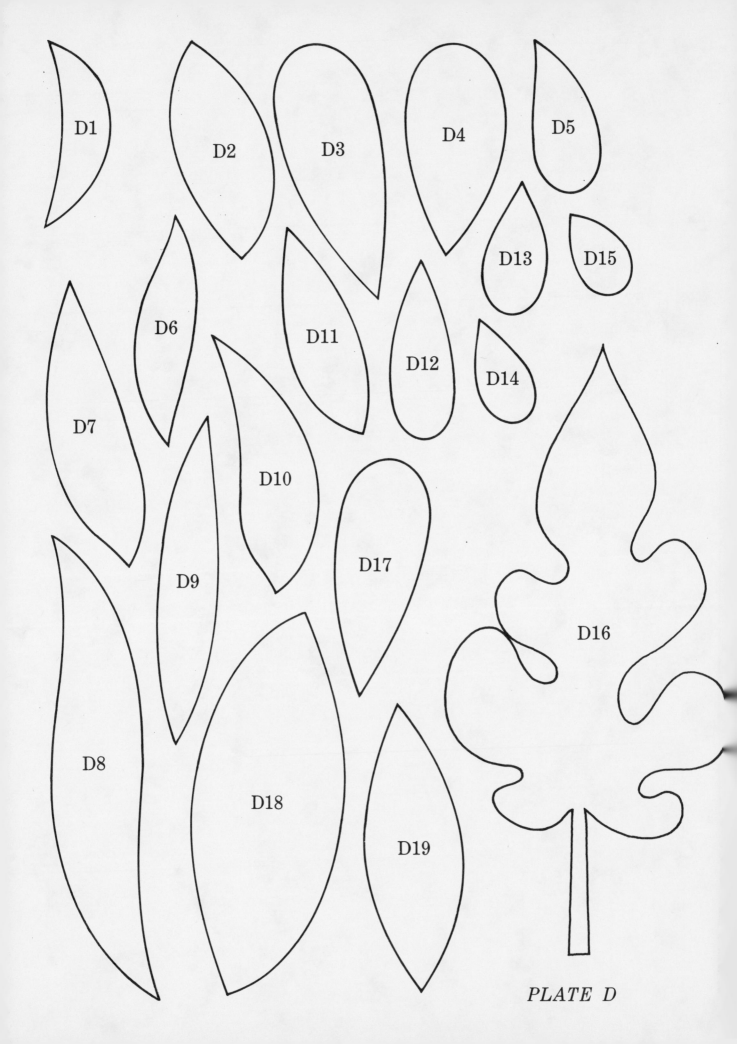

PLATE D

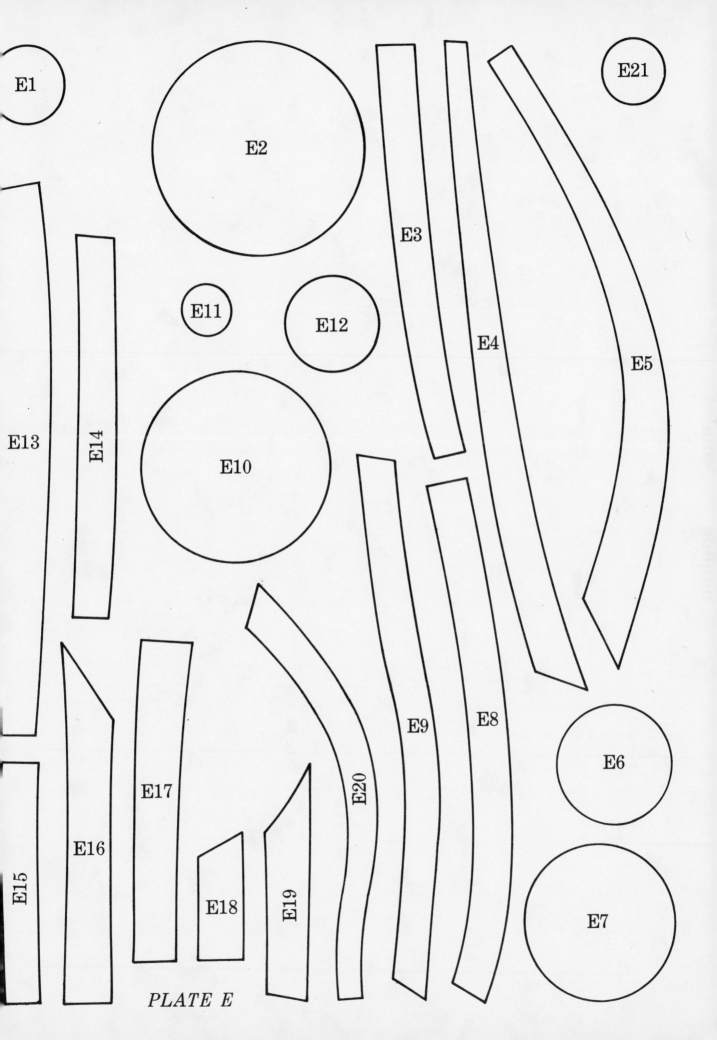

PLATE E

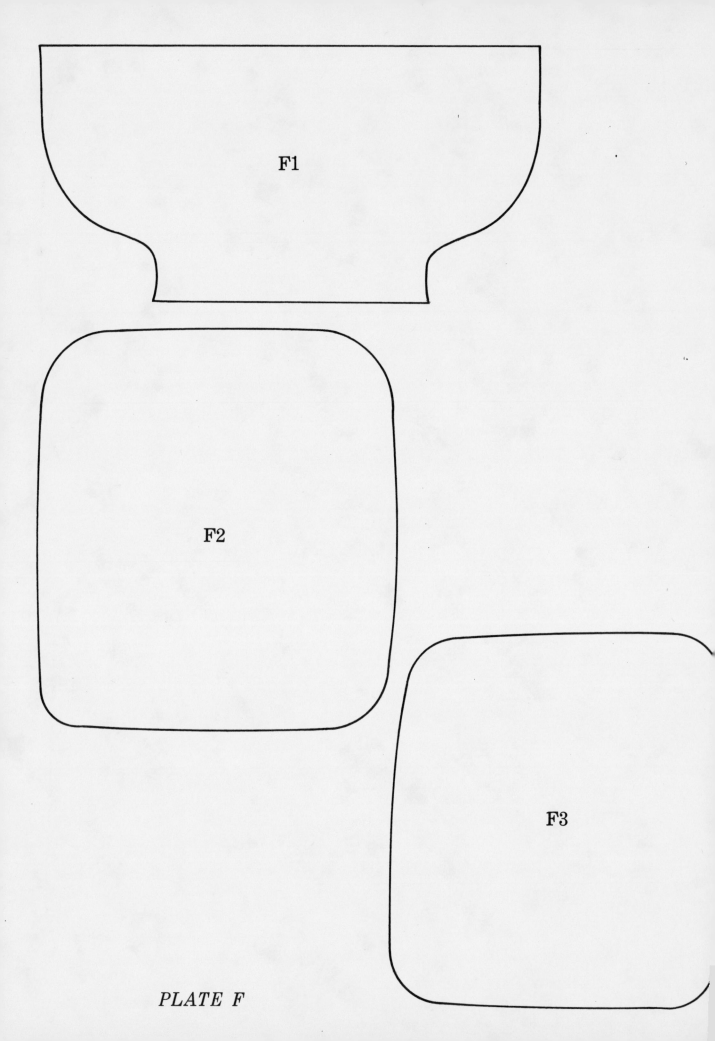

F1

F2

F3

PLATE F

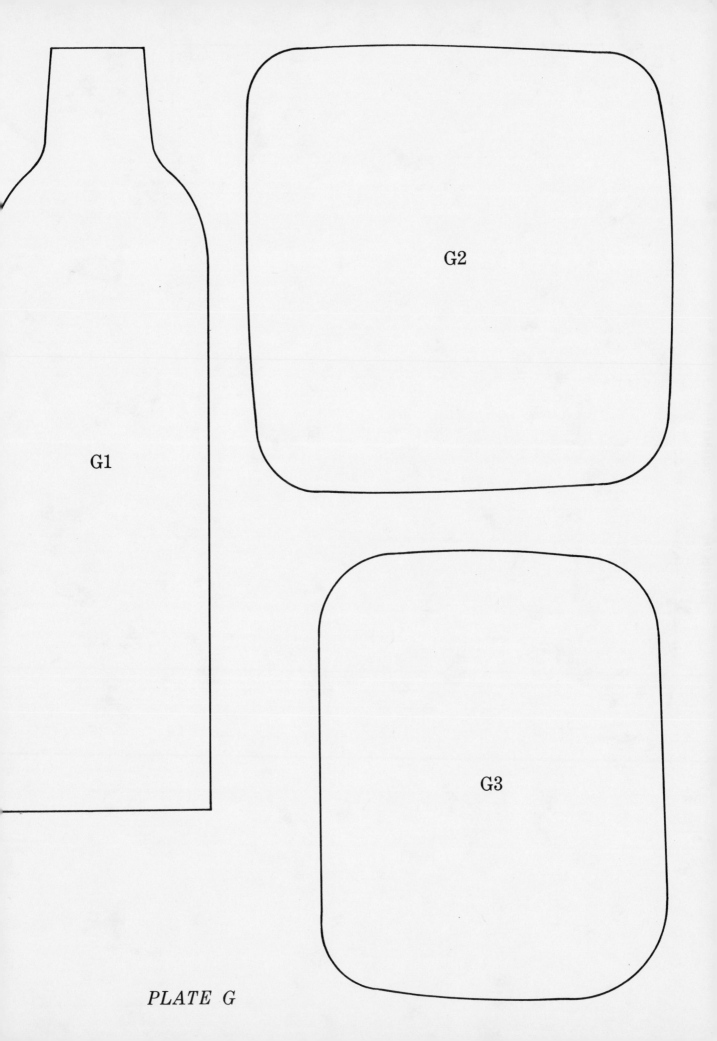

G1

G2

G3

PLATE G

PLATE H

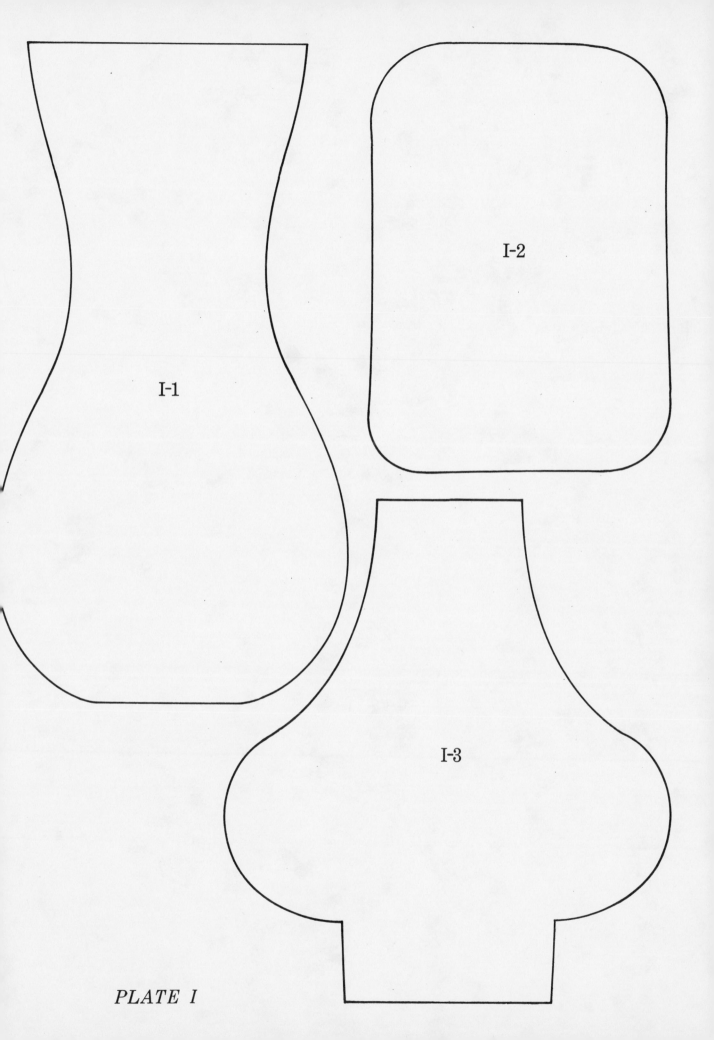

I-1

I-2

I-3

PLATE I

PLATE J

K1

K2

K3

K4

PLATE K

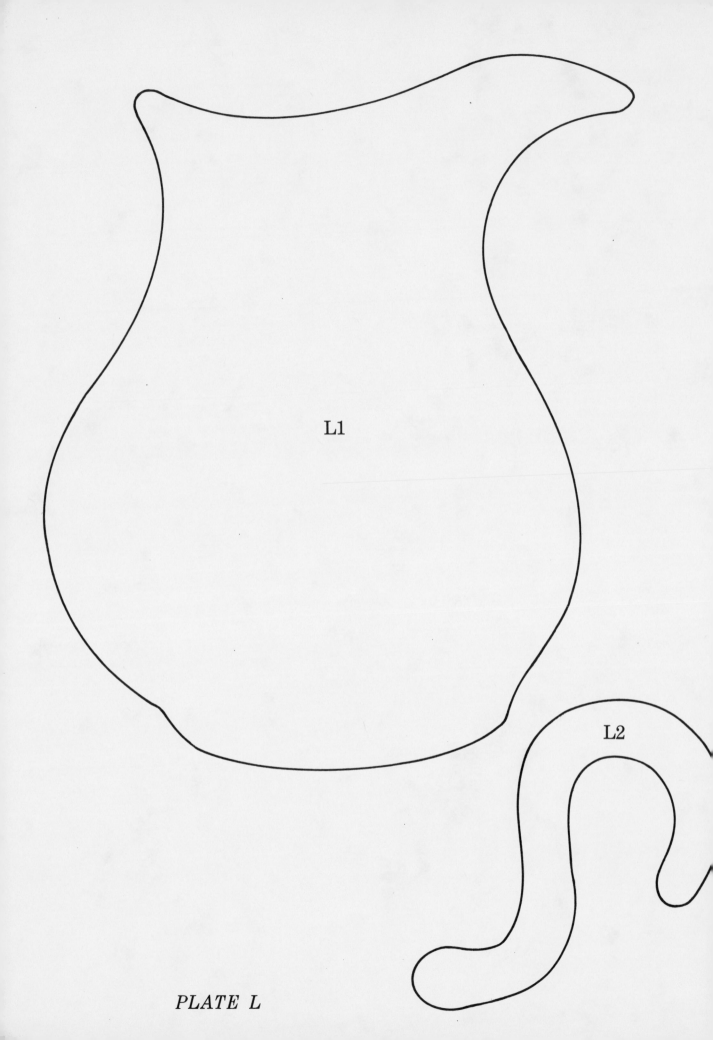

L1

L2

PLATE L

was done entirely with a running stitch. This works up very quickly, and the entire appliqué piece was done in about one hour.

4. If there are shapes which are to be overlapped, the shapes that are underneath should be completed first so that there is a neat, unbroken line at the top.

5. Parts of the design which are too small to be cut and applied to the background, such as stems, leaf veins, and the like, are indicated by the use of embroidery stitches, especially chain and stem stitch.

6. Press very carefully when finished to eliminate bumps.

(METHOD II)

All shapes are cut without seam allowances. First, follow steps 1 and 2 under Method I.

3. The pieces are permanently anchored to the background with a sewing-machine embroidery stitch (see special instructions below on using the sewing machine) or with a closed buttonhole stitch by hand. The closed buttonhole is the only hand stitch that can be used with this method because it provides an edge that will stop any fabric from fraying. Then follow steps 4, 5 and 6 of Method I to complete.

Using the Sewing Machine

The modern zigzag sewing machine can be used for appliqué embroidery. You may leave the presser foot on the machine or remove it. In either case there is no necessity for basting, as the presser foot will ride easily over the pins. If the presser foot is removed, always lower or engage the presser-foot lever or bar to insure proper tension. Open and closed satin stitch are most often used together with straight stitch and chain. Using the machine without the presser foot allows for a wider range of treatment, as it is easy to make scallops, loops, and so forth, on the various appliquéd shapes without moving the needle. Check your sewing machine instruction booklet for other information on proper settings for individual machines.

Working with Delicate Fabrics

Fabrics that fray easily when cut are *usually* not suitable for appliqué. They can, however, be used if either of the following precautions are taken.

1. Cut the shape with seam allowance, and spread a thin coating of fast-drying glue along the cut edges of the reverse side. Do not allow any of the glue to extend past the seam allowance. When dry, turn under the seam allowance and apply the shape to the background fabric.

2. Spread fast-drying glue or paste onto muslin or fine tissue paper. Place the fabric, from which you will cut the shapes, onto the glue or paste and smooth it quickly to get rid of air bubbles. Cover the pasted fabric with clean paper and weight it down with a heavy object until it is dry. Proceed to cut out the shape according to the instructions given above, applying it to the background by either Method I or Method II.

Embroidery Stitches

While this book is not intended to be a dictionary of embroidery stitches, here are some embroidery stitches which you may find helpful as you work through your designs. A combination of several different stitches always adds interest to a design. If your embroidery techniques are not the best, do not be concerned. Creativity and originality of technique are more important in appliqué embroidery than absolutely perfect stitches.

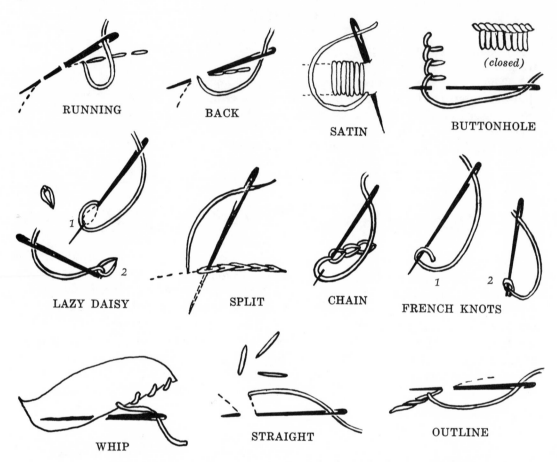

RUNNING   BACK   SATIN   BUTTONHOLE

LAZY DAISY   SPLIT   CHAIN   FRENCH KNOTS

WHIP   STRAIGHT   OUTLINE

Washing the Appliquéd Embroidery

If you have used washable materials of the same texture, you will be able to wash your appliqué embroidery. Wash gently by hand and rinse thoroughly. Remove excess moisture by rolling the embroidery in a turkish towel for about ten minutes or until it is half dry. Allow to dry flat.

If you must iron the embroidery, do so very gently on the reverse side so as not to flatten the stitches. Since you have to contend with different surface qualities in the appliqué, do not push the iron along, but lift the iron to press each bit of appliqué separately.

Diagram for appliqué appearing on front cover. Size of finished appliqué: 14″ x 19″.

Diagram for appliqué appearing on inside front cover. Size of finished appliqué: 14″ x 19″.

Diagram for appliqué appearing on inside back cover. Size of finished appliqué: 14″ x 19″.

Diagram for appliqué appearing on inside back cover. Size of finished appliqué: 14″ x 19″.

Diagram for appliqué appearing on inside back cover. Size of finished appliqué: 14″ x 19″.

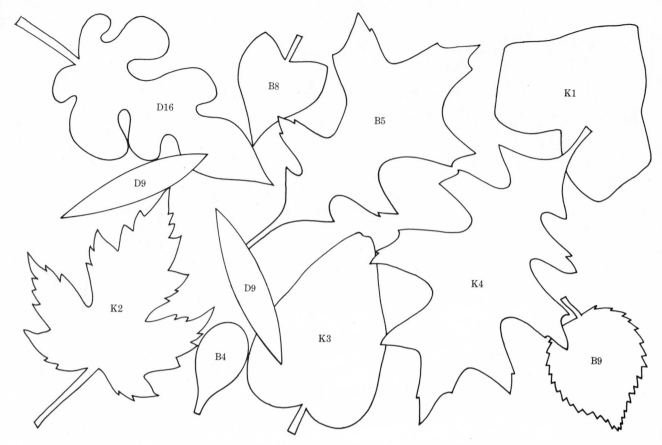

Diagram for appliqué appearing on back cover. Size of finished appliqué: 8¾″ x 13½.

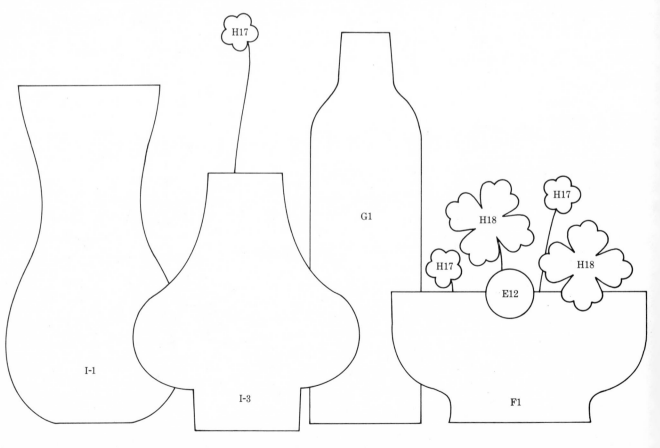

Diagram for appliqué appearing on back cover. Size of finished appliqué: 8¾″ x 13½″.